HIS
Prayer Book and Journal
For Future Spouse

Kadeen Dobbs

PUBLISHERS

ISBN: 978-1-953759-88-7 (paperback)

Dedication

For my future wife, we have not met yet, but God has made an excellent choice.

Acknowledgments

I want to first acknowledge God, who has taught me the power of praying back His holy Word to Him while waiting.

I also want to thank the DayeLight Publishing Team who has made it possible for my book to be published and read by millions of readers I will never meet, but who will meet me through my words. I pray you are transformed for God's glory.

Table of Contents

Preface

Adam was in the Garden of Eden. God observed and stated in Genesis 2:18, *"Now the Lord God said, "It is not good (beneficial) for the man to be alone; I will make him a helper [one who balances him—a counterpart who is] suitable and complementary for him." (AMP).*

God created a man to find his wife. God realized that as a social being the animals were not enough to keep Adam's company, so He fashioned a woman to meet Adam's earthly needs. Proverbs 18:22 states: *"He who finds a [true and faithful] wife finds a good thing and obtains favor and approval from the Lord." (AMP).*

Do you want to find your good thing? Do you desire marriage now or someday? Have you been married before and desire such a union again?

As you begin the journey to pray specifically for your spouse, God's best, do not underestimate the power of prayer. As you begin to pray, I encourage you to do the following:

1. Believe in Jesus, the Son of God, and His Heavenly Father.

2. Have no doubt that your prayer has already been answered.
3. Forgive everyone and pray with a clean heart and clear conscience.

Add your own. Is there a specific way you desire to be loved, to be shown affection, to feel appreciated? Are there special attributes/characteristics that you want your future spouse to possess in order to believe for your marriage to be a success?

Pray and ask the Lord for it. Write down your prayer. Be as specific as possible and say it and trust God that it will come to pass.

"Therefore I say unto you, What things soever ye desire, when ye pray, believe that ye receive them, and ye shall have them." (Mark 11:24 - KJV).

"And whatsoever ye shall ask in my name, that will I do, that the Father may be glorified in the Son. If ye shall ask any thing in my name, I will do it." (John 14:13-14 - KJV).

As you pray, be reminded that no one is perfect, and that includes you. Focus on these prayers not just as characteristics, qualities, or attributes that your spouse will develop before she meets you, but perhaps even develop while married to you. These are qualities you can continue praying for even after and during marriage. In addition, these are attributes that if you see missing in you that you can work and pray on developing because marriage is a partnership.

However, in the meantime, her mind, body and spirit is being groomed and nurtured by the Most High God in preparation of being the best spouse humanly possible for you and to you. God determined your worth when He sent His only Son to die for you. You are undeniably priceless. What can you trade a life for? Nothing. The breath in your lungs was paid for with Jesus' blood, therefore, not any partner will do; she has to be special, just like you, so wait. It will be worth it in the end.

Better to marry late than too soon and live with regret all the days of your life.

Better to marry God's pick than yours.

Better not to marry at all and live happily alone than marry and live in misery with another.

Wait, I say, wait on the Lord.

Day 1

Understanding

Scripture reference:
"Whoever is slow to anger has great understanding, but he who has a hasty temper exalts folly." (Proverbs 14:29 – ESV).

Dear Heavenly Father,

Bless me with a wife who has a heart of understanding, who is willing to open up and listen without judgment and accusations. May she appreciate my weaknesses and listen to understand, rather than listen to reply. Let our conversations at all times be gracious and pleasant. May we weigh our words so that we know how to speak and respond to each other. I pray, God, that You will grant us understanding in how to please each other, not just sexually but emotionally, intellectually, and socially in everything, and that we will keep our tongues from speaking rudely to each other and our lips from speaking deceit.

Give me understanding, God, as well as my wife, so our home can be a peaceful dwelling place.

God, may my future wife and I not lean on our own understanding but rather Yours to lead us. Even though my wife is the weaker vessel, help me, God, to be a husband who does not take advantage of her weaknesses by exercising my strength through force, and thoughtless, selfish actions that demonstrate folly and not wisdom, in Jesus' name. Amen.

Add your prayer points and scripture/s here:

_____

_____

_____

_____

_____

_____

_____

_____

_____

_____

_____

_____

_____

Day 2

Kindness

Scripture reference:
"Nothing is more appealing than speaking beautiful, life-giving words. For they release sweetness to our souls and inner healing to our spirits." (Proverbs 16:24 – TPT).

Dear Heavenly Father,

Help my wife to be good and kind to me as I will to her. You have given us the gift of free will so kindness is a choice. Help my future wife then, mighty God, to always choose kindness. Help me to reciprocate her kindness with words and deeds that show my gratitude and appreciation. Help my future wife and I to still be kind to each other even after a disagreement, and may our reactions not be spiteful and vindictive. May we bloom and blossom in our marriage as our words to each other create a healthy, happy, and loving atmosphere. As we speak kindly to each other, may we speak kindly about ourselves. Help us to utter words about ourselves that are positive, uplifting, and encouraging. May we do meaningful activities together as a couple, taking into consideration what the other enjoys doing, so compromise without complaining, in Jesus' name. Amen.

Add your prayer points and scripture/s here:

_____

_____

_____

_____

_____

_____

_____

_____

_____

_____

_____

_____

_____

_____

_____

_____

_____

Day 3

Feminine And Ladylike

Scripture reference:
"An excellent wife who can find? She is far more precious than jewels. The heart of her husband trusts in her, and he will have no lack of gain. She does him good, and not harm, all the days of her life." (Proverbs 31:10-12 - ESV).

Dear Heavenly Father,

Please bless me with a woman who isn't afraid to show her femininity. In a world where women often lead, may my wife still maintain her softness, vulnerability, and ladylike qualities while still being strong.

May she possess nurturance, gentleness, modesty, humility, compassion, helpfulness, be devoted, polite, and patient. May her inner beauty outshine her outer beauty.

May her caring nature and loyalty be appreciated by me and returned with respect and love, in Jesus' name. Amen.

Add your prayer points and scripture/s here:

_____

_____

_____

_____

_____

_____

_____

_____

_____

_____

_____

_____

_____

_____

_____

_____

_____

_____

Day 4

Loving

Scripture reference:
"With all humility and gentleness, with patience, bearing with one another in love, eager to maintain the unity of the Spirit in the bond of peace." (Ephesians 4:2-3 - ESV).

Dear Heavenly Father,

God, I know my future wife can never love me the way You do, not even close, but as much as is humanly possible, I desire a wife who is not afraid to show her affection towards me through hugs, kisses, thoughtful actions, pleasant surprises, date nights, spending quality time together, honest, and open communication. Help us to love each other without reserve and with selflessness, and to offer joy and happiness not just during times of sadness. Perfection is impossible, but loving me, who I am, must be authentic and so palpable it can be felt without touching. You are love, God, so how can You not bless me with love? Your Word says in 1 Corinthians 16:14: *"Do everything in love."* I pray then, God, that You

21

will bless me with a spouse with whom I can do EVERYTHING IN love and WITH love, in Jesus' name. Amen.

Add your prayer points and scripture/s here:

_____

_____

_____

_____

_____

_____

_____

_____

_____

_____

_____

_____

_____

_____

_____

_____

_____

Day 5

Faithfulness/Loyalty/Commitment

Scripture reference:
"Whoever finds a wife finds a good thing, and obtains favor of Yahweh." (Proverbs 18:22 – WEB).

Dear Heavenly Father,

While I wait for my spouse, I choose to pray, God, because Your Word says that he who finds a wife finds a good thing and obtains favor from the Lord. I desire a wife who will be faithful to me as I will be to her. I pray, God, that if she has any spiritual issues that relates to the lust of the flesh that You will remove such ungodly desires so that when our flesh becomes one, there is no lingering or invasion of another man in our marital bed through her mind, thoughts, spirit, and body. Let her be loyal, not just physically but verbally. May she not discuss me with anyone but choose to resolve disagreements about me with me. Let her sexual appetite be fulfilled by only me, her husband, that she will have no desire to seek out the attention or affection of another man for emotional,

social, physical, or sexual fulfillment, in Jesus' name.
Amen.

Add your prayer points and scripture/s here:

_____

_____

_____

_____

_____

_____

_____

_____

_____

_____

_____

_____

_____

_____

_____

_____

_____

_____

Day 6

Trust/Confidentiality

Scripture reference:

"A gossip betrays a confidence, but a trustworthy person keeps a secret." (Proverbs 11:13 – NIV).

Dear Heavenly Father,

Bless me with a wife with whom I can share my secrets and not have it thrown back in my face when there is an argument—a woman with whom I can show my vulnerability and open up to without fear of being judged or mistreated. Bless me with a wife with whom when affairs are discussed will remain private.

May we connect as friends and actually enjoy socializing to and with each other. May we trust each other enough to see each other as the first person to confide in, in times of need and discomfort. May she not seek validation from anyone and have a healthy sense of loyalty, so we speak the truth to each other in a loving way. May she be an active listener who gives and takes sound advice, in Jesus' name. Amen.

Add your prayer points and scripture/s here:

_____

_____

_____

_____

_____

_____

_____

_____

_____

_____

_____

_____

_____

_____

_____

_____

_____

_____

_____

_____

_____

Day 7

Godliness/Prays

Scripture reference:

For bodily exercise profiteth little: but godliness is profitable unto all things, having promise of the life that now is, and of that which is to come. (1 Timothy 4:8 - KJV).

Dear Heavenly Father,

Your Word says that two cannot walk unless they agree. God, grant me a wife with whom I can read the Bible daily with, discuss the Word of God with, and learn from each other and grow together spiritually. I pray, God, that she possesses an intrinsic desire and motivation to read the Word of God and encourage me as I will do for her. Help my future wife to not just be a hearer of the Word but a doer. Let her daily walk exemplify the Word and instructions of God. Let her not practice the Word of God to be noticed by others, but let her godliness be a genuine relationship between herself and her Creator. I pray that as we grow spiritually, that our emotional attachment will also be strengthened for as we dwell under the shadow of the Almighty, we will abide in our home, together, in peace, harmony, and love. Let God be the center of our union and marriage as we spend time in His presence daily. Let it indeed be holy matrimony, in Jesus' name. Amen.

Add your prayer points and scripture/s here:

_____

_____

_____

_____

_____

_____

_____

_____

_____

_____

_____

_____

_____

_____

_____

_____

_____

Day 8

Trust In My Capabilities

Scripture reference:
"But I want you to understand that the head of every man is Christ, the head of a wife is her husband, and the head of Christ is God." (1 Corinthians 11:3 - ESV).

Dear Heavenly Father,

Please bless me with a wife who allows me to be the head of the household and to lead with love and respect. Let her tongue not be quick to belittle and emasculate my masculinity. May she trust that I can and will take care of her and protect her to the best of my ability. May I exceed her expectations without having to feel that I must exert and overdo to please or become someone I am not.

Let trust come as I demonstrate and prove that I am worthy and deserving of it. Help me, Lord, to never give her a reason to doubt my sincerity or honesty. May my actions to earn her trust be rewarded with acceptance, appreciation, and gratitude, in Jesus' name. Amen.

Add your prayer points and scripture/s here:

_____

_____

_____

_____

_____

_____

_____

_____

_____

_____

_____

_____

_____

_____

_____

_____

_____

_____

_____

_____

_____

_____

Day 9

Not Talkative/A Gossiper

Scripture reference:
"There are six evils God truly hates and a seventh that is an abomination to him: Putting others down while considering yourself superior, spreading lies and rumors, spilling the blood of the innocent, plotting evil in your heart toward another, gloating over doing what's plainly wrong, spouting lies in false testimony, and stirring up strife between friends. These are entirely despicable to God!" (Proverbs 6:16-19 - TPT).

Dear Heavenly Father,

I pray that my wife has none of the above that You so despise.

Your Word states that a gossiper betrays confidence, but a trustworthy person keeps a secret. Bless my future wife with the ability to restrain her tongue from speaking about others and our marriage. Let her feet not be quick to run to spread slander and deceit or her fingers quick to dial to spill the latest juicy details. Let her not take delight in spreading false reports and stirring up conflict and drama. The tongue has the power of life and death, so help my wife and I to use our tongues to speak life and thus reap the fruits of what we speak which are love, kindness, gentleness, encouraging and uplifting words that build and not destroy one's self-esteem. May what we speak benefit others and, if it isn't worth saying, then give us, mighty God, the restraint to exercise silence, in Jesus' name. Amen.

Add your prayer points and scripture/s here:

_____

_____

_____

_____

_____

_____

_____

_____

_____

_____

_____

_____

Day 10

Appreciation And Affirmation

Scripture reference:
"Gracious words are like a honeycomb, sweetness to the soul and health to the body." (Proverbs 16:24 - NLT).

Dear Heavenly Father,

Please bless me with a spouse who is appreciative of the things I will do to make our home one of peace and love. May the things I do be reciprocated with positive gestures or verbal declarations of emotional support or encouragement. May we treasure the moments we spend together and look forward to doing things for each other. May there be a balance of give and take, and may what we do for each other not be done with resentment and bitterness. Let there be genuine thankfulness and may we live a life honouring each other and our marriage, in Jesus' name. Amen.

Add your prayer points and scripture/s here:

Day 11

Respect

Scripture reference:

"Do nothing from selfishness or empty conceit, but with humility consider one another as more important than yourselves." (Philippians 2:3 - NASB).

Dear Heavenly Father,

Bless me with a wife who is respectful enough to be honest and open about her feelings, has manners, and is polite. When angry, may she not resort to expletives to get her point across or throw low blows in an attempt to damage my manhood and self-esteem. Help me too, God, to give her the respect she needs by making sure she never feels less than a woman or my partner by being unfaithful. May I establish and maintain respectful boundaries with female co-workers and friends, so my loyalty is never questioned. I also expect too, God, that what I give will be returned as respect is earned. May we not take pleasure in gloating if the other is wrong and may my past and hers stay there—in the past. May her respect be extended to my family and vice versa, in Jesus' name. Amen.

Add your prayer points and scripture/s here:

_____

_____

_____

_____

_____

_____

_____

_____

_____

_____

_____

_____

_____

_____

_____

_____

_____

_____

Day 12

Friendship/ Companionship

Scripture reference:
"Better is open rebuke than hidden love. Wounds from a friend can be trusted, but an enemy multiplies kisses." (Proverbs 27:5-6 - NIV).

Dear Heavenly Father,

A good friend listens, has your back and is someone who can keep a secret. Also, a good friend is someone with whom you can have a good time, even when you are doing absolutely nothing. Likewise, a good friend tells you the truth no matter what, is non-judgmental, is empathic and sympathetic, generous, encouraging, and supportive. For these reasons, I pray, God, that I will find an excellent friend in my future wife.

It is loving to receive rebuke when necessary because correction and constructive suggestions build trust. Good friends communicate, so may the dialogue between us occur like two friends who choose to marry

41

and experience holy, beautiful matrimony, in Jesus' name. Amen.

Add your prayer points/ scriptures here:

_____

_____

_____

_____

_____

_____

_____

_____

_____

_____

_____

_____

_____

_____

_____

_____

_____

_____

Day 13

Peaceful/Not Quarrelsome

Scripture reference:

"It is better to live in a corner of the housetop than in a house shared with a quarrelsome wife." (Proverbs 21:9 - ESV).

Dear Heavenly Father,

Choose a future wife for me, one who is not argumentative, must have the final word, and who believes she is never wrong. Let our days in private and public be peaceful. May my wife be agreeable, easy to get along with, while still remaining one who is not easily taken advantage of. May she know the difference between standing up for herself and being argumentative. May she know the difference between being aggressive and being assertive, stating a point or being disrespectful and rude.

Teach us to gauge our words, for death and life are in the power of the tongue, and thus, life or death are in our spoken words, in Jesus' name. Amen.

Add your prayer points and scripture/s here:

_____

_____

_____

_____

_____

_____

_____

_____

_____

_____

_____

_____

_____

_____

_____

_____

_____

_____

_____

_____

Day 14

Wise

Scripture reference:

"If any of you lacks wisdom, let him ask of God, who gives to all liberally and without reproach, and it will be given to him." (James 1:5 - NKJV).

Dear Heavenly Father,

I pray that You will bless my future wife liberally with wisdom. May she possess the qualities of having experience, knowledge, and good judgment without being arrogant or cocky. As I, and others, confide in her, help her to offer helpful and solid advice. May she offer instruction humbly, be an active listener and live with purpose and accept ALL of me for who I am. The Word of God says that fools despise wisdom and instruction, so as my wife gives wise advice, may I in turn be able to receive it with grace. May she be open to reasoning, full of mercy, be impartial, and sincere. Remind her daily that she can never come close to being as wise as you. May she not be reckless and careless but cautious and find evil not in the least appealing. Help us to be tactful in our conversations and the manner in which we respond to each other. May she always hold herself accountable before you, God, in Jesus' name. Amen.

Add your prayer points and scripture/s here:

_____

_____

_____

_____

_____

_____

_____

_____

_____

_____

_____

_____

_____

_____

_____

_____

_____

Day 15

Hard Worker

Scripture reference:
"Lazy hands make for poverty, but diligent hands bring wealth." (Proverbs 10:4 - NIV).

Dear Heavenly Father,

As the man, I know it is my job to provide, but your Word says two hands are better than one, for the success and profit are greater because we toil together. Bless me with a wife who does not mind working if she has to and appreciates the value of money. Let her not be a spendthrift or a lover of money, which is the root of all evil, but rather wise in her spending habits.

Give us diligent hands, so we make the most of every opportunity according to Your will. Help us to work heartily unto You and not unto men. Give us the strength to do what we must for Your Kingdom and show us how to work smart to make the very best use of our gifts and talents for Your glory, in Jesus' name. Amen.

Add your prayer and scripture/s here:

_____

_____

_____

_____

_____

_____

_____

_____

_____

_____

_____

_____

_____

_____

_____

_____

_____

_____

Day 16

Good Listener/Independent Thinker

Scripture reference:
"Know this, my beloved brothers: let every person be quick to hear, slow to speak, slow to anger." (James 1:19 - ESV).

Dear Heavenly Father,

Help my wife and I to speak evil of no one, to avoid quarreling, to be gentle, and to show courtesy toward all people. Help us be slow in offering advice, slow in reacting, and not be quick to interrupt others who are speaking, not jump to conclusions or make judgments prematurely, and to be easily distracted by worldly opinions, ideologies, and philosophies. May she not be easily influenced by friends to do what is wrong or change her conduct to fit in. May we stay rooted in Your Word and not be of this world though in it. May our thought-process and, hence, our decisions be influenced by You, Mighty God, in Jesus' name. Amen.

Add your own prayer and scripture/s here:

_____

_____

_____

_____

_____

_____

_____

_____

_____

_____

_____

_____

_____

_____

_____

_____

_____

_____

_____

_____

Day 17

Intimacy

Scripture reference:
"Do not deprive one another, except perhaps by agreement for a limited time, that you may devote yourselves to prayer; but then come together again, so that Satan may not tempt you because of your lack of self-control." (1 Corinthians 7:5 - ESV).

Dear Heavenly Father,

Mighty God, Your Word says in 1 Corinthians 7:3 that a husband must give his wife conjugal visits, and likewise the wife. The marital bed is undefiled, so help us not to deny each other the pleasure of each other's body and to do always as husband and wife what is honorable in Your sight. May we experience not just a physical connection, but also an emotional one. In our bedroom may there be mutual care, trust, and acceptance. May our intimacy transcend the bedroom, and may we also experience mental and spiritual intimacy. As we embark on adventures and day-to-day occurrences and happenings, may we also experience creative and experiential intimacy and thus our intimate connectivity will be holistic. May we know when to give each other space without feeling rejected, dejected, insecure and needy. May we learn how to make each other feel special, so intimacy is maintained even when apart, in Jesus' name. Amen.

Add your prayer points and scripture/s here:

_____

_____

_____

_____

_____

_____

_____

_____

_____

_____

_____

_____

_____

_____

_____

Day 18

Not Manipulative

Scripture reference:

"Love is patient and kind; love does not envy or boast; it is not arrogant or rude. It does not insist on its own way; it is not irritable or resentful; it does not rejoice at wrongdoing, but rejoices with the truth. Love bears all things, believes all things, hopes all things, endures all things." (1 Corinthians 13:4-7 - ESV).

Dear Heavenly Father,

Please bless me with a wife who finds deception distasteful and does not enjoy playing the victim. May she not be controlling and pretentious. May she be sincere in all that she does and be blessed with a humble spirit. May she find no delight in another's demise and take advantage of my love for her.

May what I give, which is fairness and honesty without malicious intent, be reciprocated, in Jesus' name. Amen.

Add your prayer points and scripture/s here:

_____

_____

_____

_____

_____

_____

_____

_____

_____

_____

_____

_____

_____

_____

_____

_____

_____

_____

_____

_____

_____

_____

Day 19

Say "I Love You"

Scripture reference:

"Dear children, let's not merely say that we love each other; let us show the truth by our actions." (1 John 3:18 - NLT).

Dear Heavenly Father,

Just as a woman loves to hear the words "I love you," so does a man love to hear the same from the woman he has chosen to open up to, show his affections, and confess his undying love. May this declaration of love strengthen our union and intimacy, physically, emotionally, mentally, spiritually, and socially. May this truth be evident in our communication and treatment of each other. May we be vocal in expressing as such even after a disagreement and mean it because love can cover a multitude of sins, in Jesus' name. Amen.

Add your prayer points and scripture/s here:

_____

_____

Day 20

Humility

Scripture reference:

"But He gives us more and more grace [through the power of the Holy Spirit to defy sin and live an obedient life that reflects both our faith and our gratitude for our salvation]. Therefore, it says, "God is opposed to the proud and haughty, but [continually] gives [the gift of] grace to the humble [who turn away from self-righteousness]."" (James 4:6 - AMP).

Dear Heavenly Father,

Clothe my future wife with humility. Help her to understand that God opposes the proud but shows favour to the humble, and if she humbles herself before You, mighty God, she will be lifted up. Make my future wife aware that with pride comes disgrace, but with humility comes wisdom; with a haughty heart comes downfall, but with humility comes honour. When someone praises her, may she accept such compliments with modesty. May she possess manners and not hesitate to say "thank you" when necessary. May she acknowledge when she has received assistance and not bask in the praise, deliberately omitting and pretending that her accomplishments were done independently. May she be comfortable sharing the spotlight and, when eyes are not on her, NOT feel inclined to do deeds and say words for the sole purpose of making her the center of attention. Is there such a woman? I believe so, mighty God, and I know You have already blessed me with her. So, thank You in advance, in Jesus' name. Amen.

Add your prayer points and scripture/s here:

_____

_____

_____

_____

_____

_____

_____

_____

_____

_____

_____

_____

_____

Day 21

Forgiving

Scripture reference:
"Be angry [at sin—at immorality, at injustice, at ungodly behavior], yet do not sin; do not let your anger [cause you shame, nor allow it to] last until the sun goes down." (Ephesians 4:26 – AMP).

Dear Heavenly Father,

Your Word instructs in Ephesians 4:26 that the sun should not set upon our anger, so, Heavenly Father, I desire a spouse with whom I will never retire or go to sleep filled with anger and malice. May we learn to forgive each other as Christ has forgiven us and become stronger because of our differences. May we resolve conflicts by watching our tone and volume of voice and not being too proud to apologize to each other as often as is necessary. Help us to choose the right timing and words that will not add fuel to our disagreement and thus set it ablaze, but rather listen to each other's perspective with openness and possess a willingness to "squash" each argument with a "kiss," "I love you" or in prayer as we realize that as husband and wife we are now one flesh and what hurts one, hurts the other, so each issue must be addressed and resolved with LOVE.

Add your prayer points and scripture/s here:

_____

_____

_____

_____

_____

_____

_____

_____

_____

_____

_____

_____

_____

_____

_____

_____

_____

_____

_____

Bonus

Day 22

Not Envious And Jealous

Scripture references:
"A calm and peaceful and tranquil heart is life and health to the body, but passion and envy are like rottenness to the bones." (Proverbs 14:30 - AMP).

"For where jealousy and selfish ambition exist, there is disorder [unrest, rebellion] and every evil thing and morally degrading practice." (James 3:16 - AMP).

Dear Heavenly Father,

Please bless my spouse with the ability to not see others and feel discontent and believe that they are undeserving of their successes and instead it should be her. Grant her the grace to be happy for others and content with what she has, understanding that God can and will bless her with the desires of her heart as she waits with patience and in God's will according to His perfect timing. Help her not to fret

70

when people succeed in their wicked schemes, for Your Word instructs and encourages in Psalm 37:1: ***"Do not worry because of evildoers, nor be envious toward wrongdoers."*** Help her in all things to rejoice, be thankful and grateful and understand that this is the will of God for her life and that circumstances disliked can and will change and work out for her good, in Jesus' name. Amen.

Add your prayer points and scripture/s here:

_____

_____

_____

_____

_____

_____

_____

_____

_____

_____

_____

_____

_____

_____

_____

Love Affirmations

In my book titled "21 Powerful and Practical Things to Do While Waiting To Be Wed," I shared some biblical affirmations which are in audio form on my YouTube Channel (Kadeen Dobbs).

Here is a space for you to create your own AFFIRMATIONS as you wait for your future spouse.

_____

_____

_____

_____

_____

_____

_____

_____

_____

_____

_____

_____

_____

Love Quotes

Here are a few love quotes that I have created for myself.

"LOVE IS FROM GOD. LUST IS FROM SATAN."

"LOVE IS PUTTING SOMEONE ELSE'S
NEEDS BEFORE YOURS." —OLAF

"LOVE WILL FIND A WAY WITH GOD'S HELP."

"Don't always follow your heart.
Instead, always follow God's
voice."

'LOVE DOES MEAN HAVING TO SAY "I'M SORRY."'

"If you lose your morals while in LOVE, then it isn't love, it's a LIABILITY."

"If she constantly hurts you, then her LOVE for you is a feeling NOT an emotion."

"SOMETIMES LOVE lost and
UNREQUITED IS SIMULTANEOUSLY
REMEDY AND THERAPY."

Add your LOVE quotes here:

Lessons Learnt From a Broken Heart

Write what you learnt from experiencing heartbreak. Were there any red flags that you ignored? Did you put up with situations that now that you are out of it and waiting for God's best, you realize the error in your behaviours?

Write these down as reminders of what you learnt and will not tolerate again.

_____

_____

_____

_____

_____

_____

_____

_____

_____

_____

_____

Relationship Goals

Make your own relationship goals. Social media has a way of presenting "perfect couples" who are sometimes idolized and envied. Do not let that be you. Create your own and let God place in your heart what you need in a spouse as opposed to what you want. Let God lead you. Trust in His divine understanding and matchmaking skills.

_____

_____

_____

_____

_____

_____

_____

_____

_____

_____

_____

_____

_____

About the Author

Kadeen Dobbs' innate passion to write stems from a love of the Godhead. She is a teacher who has taught varying age groups across the educational spectrum and in different countries from kindergarteners to adults. Kadeen also blogs. Her website is: http://kadeendobbs.wixsite.com/soaringtomynewbeginn. Her blogs explore and discuss a plethora of topics from a spiritual perspective, through the lens of her experiences.

Her intrinsic desire for imparting knowledge has transcended beyond the classroom and has prompted her to write and publish her written works. In addition, her YouTube channel "Kadeen Dobbs" has biblical affirmations to listen and declare that uplift, encourage, empower, and motivate men and women. Kadeen is active in her Ministry and has been featured in magazines in Jamaica, the Caribbean, and the USA.

Kadeen LOVES to travel, and it is her desire, as the future unfolds, to visit all seven continents. Follow her on Instagram:

https://www.instagram.com/dobbskadeen/
for more inspiring content.

Made in the USA
Middletown, DE
14 June 2022

67170716R00056